Saint Padre PIO Speaks

TOME I

Saint Padre Pio Speaks: Book 1

Published by Abba Books LLC
abbabooksllc@gmail.com
Copyright © 2023 Marie-Josée Thibault

All Rights Reserved

No part of this publication may be reproduced, distributed, or transmitted in any form or by any means, including photocopying, recording, or other electronic or mechanical methods, without the prior written permission of the publisher.

First Edition, 2023
Designed and Edited by Abba Books LLC
ISBN: 979-8-9875984-3-6

Abba Books LLC
34972 Newark Blvd, #441
Newark, CA 94560

www.abbamyfatheriloveyou.com
https://www.facebook.com/AbbaILoveYouBooks/

Preface	VI
Chapter 1	9
Chapter 2	13
Chapter 3	15
Chapter 4	19
Chapter 5	23
Chapter 6	27
Chapter 7	31
Chapter 8	33
Chapter 9	37
Chapter 10	41
Chapter 11	45
Chapter 12	47
Chapter 13	51
Chapter 14	55
Chapter 15	59
Chapter 16	63

Chapter 17	67
Chapter 18	71
Chapter 19	75
Chapter 20	77
Chapter 21	79
Chapter 22	83
Chapter 23	87
Chapter 24	91
Chapter 25	95
Chapter 26	99
Chapter 27	103
Chapter 28	105
Chapter 29	109
Chapter 30	113
Chapter 31	117
Chapter 32	121

Pio is simultaneously the sweetest and the strictest Saint who visits me regularly. He was very specific about the illustrations he wanted for his book. He also gives the best "bear hug" in the whole world! Let me give you a teaser here:

"I am Saint Padre Pio and my intercession before God the Father to obtain the salvation of your soul at this point in your life is a blessing without compare among the gifts of Heaven. For the stigmata I bore on my physical body, sacred and blessed effigy of Christ Jesus who is Divine Love, are still visible on my etheric body for all to behold here."

Enjoy Pio's visitations!

Marie-Josée Thibault

FREE DOWNLOAD

Get your free copy of :
"Dear Humanity: Book 1"
when you sign up to the
author's VIP mailing list!
Get started here:

www.abbamyfatheriloveyou.com

Chapter 1

My children, I am Saint Padre Pio.

I am pleased to speak to you today through the essence of Saint Paul on earth, Marie-Josée Thibault. The situation is serious and time is short. It is urgent that you listen to me today.

The stigmata that I bore during my life on earth were an extraordinary blessing received directly from God the Father. This blessing was not only of me, but also of all those who have been saved thanks to the infinite redemption hidden within these stigmata. I wish to teach you the mysteries of the crucifixion, of the redemption, and of the salvation of your soul through the might, beauty, and reverence of the stigmata, which I still bear here in the above.

I am thankful to Christ Jesus, my Savior and my King, for giving this astounding grace: to me, a servant of God, and to you, dear reader, a soul in distress seeking God.

God loves you; and this miraculous book reaching you today is an extraordinary gift originating directly from Him, the very Source of all redemption. For God our Father is infinite mercy and infinite justice.

Alleluia! Alleluia! Alleluia! Blessed are those who are invited to learn the teaching contained within the stigmata, cosmic vessels of infinite mercy of God the Father, the Creator of us all. Amen. Alleluia!

SAINT PADRE PIO

Speaks

Chapter 2

My children, may it be very clear for you today that nothing I say unto you could be conceived by the human mind. Heavenly messages are divine, eternal, ineffable, and sanctioned by God the Father Himself, who loves you so much. Nothing I say could be invented by Marie-Josée or by any human whatsoever. For the Words that I say unto you are Holy.

I say unto you, I say unto you verily, and I repeat it unto you, that I am Saint Padre Pio. I bless you in the Name of the Father, and of the Son, and of the Holy Spirit. Amen. So be it.

Alleluia! Alleluia! Alleluia! Blessed are those who will join us here in Paradise, in the absolute joy that is life with Christ Jesus, my Savior and my God. Blessed is he who believes and who comes in the Name of the Lord. Amen. So be it.

SAINT PADRE PIO
Speaks

Chapter 3

My friends, my beloved children, I am pleased to speak to you today, for time is short and the situation on earth is precarious. You must convert to the Lord Jesus Christ, our Savior and our Heart, today, at the very moment that you are reading these lines.

I am Saint Padre Pio and my intercession before God the Father to obtain the salvation of your soul at this point in your life is a blessing without compare among the gifts of Heaven. For the stigmata I bore on my physical body, sacred and blessed effigy of Christ Jesus who is Divine Love, are still visible on my etheric body for all to behold here. Here is Paradise, home to the Saints, the pure souls, the Angels and their hierarchy, the Most Blessed Virgin Mary, Christ Jesus—our Everything—the Holy Spirit, and the Father Almighty.

My stigmata, therefore, retain a unique power even now; in fact, their powers are even more intense now, because my human nature, little and feeble, was eliminated after the passage that is death—in my case, in 1968. Consequently, my stigmata are the subject of my discourse with you, inhabitants of the earth in distress, my beloved children, a discourse conducted so that you may better understand my unique intervention in your life.

Alleluia! Alleluia! Alleluia! Blessed is he who believes in the transcendent and miraculous powers of the stigmata, sacred vehicles of the Divine and ineffable Mercy of God the Father Almighty. Amen. Alleluia!

SAINT PADRE PIO

Speaks

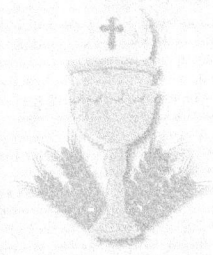

Chapter 4

My children, my children, listen to me well. I am here in Heaven with Christ, but I am also among you on earth.

The dedication to my Holiness expressed by millions of people around the world touches me and fills me with joy and gladness! I hear all your prayers and I intercede before God the Father in favour of every request presented to me.

I say unto you, I say unto you verily, that because of my sacrifice on earth, God the Father is very sensitive to the prayers that I personally present to Him. The stigmata that I still bear testify to the generosity, the goodness, and the love of God the Father toward all His children, by virtue of the mercy contained within the stigmata.

Pray, my children, pray to God the Father, and request my intercession as often as possible. For God the Father loves

you and wishes for the salvation of your soul, in virtue of His Divine and infinite Mercy.

Alleluia! Alleluia! Alleluia! Blessed are all the prayerful ones before God the Father, on earth as it is in Heaven! Amen. Alleluia!

SAINT PADRE PIO

Speaks

SAINT PADRE PIO
Speaks

Chapter 5

My children, my children, do not further delay in your inner spiritual endeavor and your return to God. Time is short! The Saints of Paradise, the Angels of God, the Legion of Saint Paul that expands day by day: we are all here around you to inspire you, to heal you, to support you, and especially to intercede before God the Father, our Creator, in the Name of Love Incarnate, who is our Lord Jesus Christ, Lord of Heaven and earth.

We rush at the very moment when our name or image appears in your mind or your heart. We perceive the full range of your emotions, we know the extent of your problems, and we hasten with joy and solicitude to present your requests and petitions to God the Father, who is Pure Love.

You need our help at this point in your journey on earth: that is why this miraculous book has reached your hands

today. Your mercy has been initiated, your salvation is at your fingertips, and the passage that is death will be peaceful and glorious if—and only if—you follow the religious rites that are taught to you by Christ Jesus, our Lord and our God.

Christ Jesus, my Lord, continually speaks to you in your heart, but the clamor that is life on earth hinders your hearing. Follow the doctrines taught in the Bible, obey the instructions given by our Lord Jesus Christ through His Apostles and His messengers over the course of human history; and, above all, read with faith and attention the books dictated to the essence of Saint Paul on earth, Marie-Josée Thibault. For shortly, very shortly, everything will be clear with regard to the genuine sincerity and dedication of this soul blessed by God the Father Himself. For the stigmata will also appear on her body. Perhaps they already have by the time you are reading these lines.

Alleluia! Alleluia! Alleluia! Blessed are the messengers of Christ on earth, tangible testimonies of the love of God the Father for all His children. Amen. So be it.

SAINT PADRE PIO

Speaks

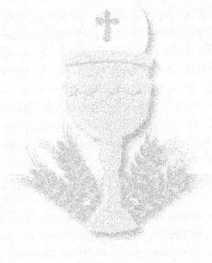

Chapter 6

My children, my children, I speak to you with mounting sadness. So much darkness on earth! So much suffering within your hearts! As we observe it from here, in Paradise, the situation among human beings is getting worse day by day.

The involution observed in the behavior of men is aberrant and tragic and must be reversed: this is why the events that are approaching are inevitable. But more importantly, these events are also desirable for the sake of reorienting the spiritual growth of human hearts.

The new civilization that is being prepared will be focused solely on Christ Savior; the destruction that is coming is necessary to make way for renewal and for the cosmic rebirth of the current civilization, which has lost itself.

Alleluia! Alleluia! Alleluia! Blessed are those who are invited to the New Sun that will rise shortly, for an era of peace, holiness, and Christic Light will replace the current era. Amen. So be it.

SAINT PADRE PIO

Speaks

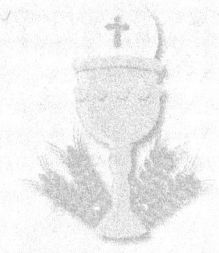

Chapter 7

My children, my beloved children, I am Saint Padre Pio. During my earthly life, I performed the sacrament of confession for the salvation of the many thousands of souls that the Absolute Father sent me.

I say unto you, I say unto you verily, that the Eternal Father directed me to you today so that I may proceed to your confession. What happiness in Paradise! For your soul will soon enter the ineffable spheres of the Kingdom of God, where only the souls purified by confession and other means of redemption can enter.

Alleluia! Alleluia! Alleluia! Blessed are those who obtain confession through this miraculous book, for their souls are preparing for the judgment of God the Father with courage, serenity, and hope in the name of Christ the Savior. Amen. Alleluia!

SAINT PADRE PIO

Speaks

Chapter 8

My children, I am with you as you are reading these lines. I, Saint Padre Pio, member of the Legion of Saint Paul, invite you to join us here in Paradise after the passage that is death; and I promise to do so today.

I say unto you, I say unto you verily, that the confession of your heart is important today. Every confession is an admission of sins before God the Father Almighty. Everything that is not of Christ, everything that is not as holy as Christ, in principle constitutes a sin, an opacity, a darkness in the Eyes of the Father.

The enormity of the sins of men on earth, considered individually and collectively, exceeds human understanding. Only Divine Grace can wash away the sins of the world, through its Gentle Lamb, the Lamb of God, Christ Jesus

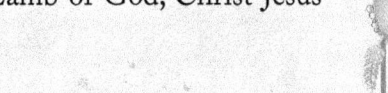

our Savior, who has executed His mission on earth to perfection.

Indeed, His life, His crucifixion, His death, His resurrection, His ascension, and the Pentecost have all allowed the crystallization of the cosmic and divine Mysteries, and justify our boundless adoration and praise for Him—for our Christ the Savior. The Mysteries here above are the key that is opening the door to the redemption of human souls, a cosmic mystery allowing for the salvation of humanity and the peaceful return of every soul to God the Father.

For sins cannot be erased without the help of Christ, the Lamb of God, the King of the world. His Name, His Majesty, His Love, His triumphant and bleeding Holy wounds, His Blood, His Body, and the Cross He bore, with compassion and forgiveness for all, have won our redemption, a cosmic mystery through which each life form has changed its course. From death arose life, Eternal life in the Kingdom of God, an Ocean of Life in Christ, forming only One, One Body in Christ.

Alleluia! Alleluia! Alleluia! Blessed are those who are invited to the communion of the mysteries of Christ, the mysteries of Eternal life that are revealed to you today! Amen. Alleluia!!

SAINT PADRE PIO

Speaks

Chapter 9

My beloved children of the earth, come into my arms! Through the gift of confession that I have, your soul will be purified and will become as white as snow! It is time to confess. My children, you must look at your life with detachment, as if it were not yours. Look at your life from the perspective of God the Father, your Creator.

What have you done with your talents? Have you explored your qualities and skills, which have been given to you thanks to God's generosity to you? Are you compassionate, charitable, patient, and sincere toward your fellow men? Are you able to control your emotions and your thoughts so as to keep your heart in a state of worthiness in the Eyes of God? Have you caused pain and suffering in others? Have you used your time on earth, which is so precious, on useless and vain projects, without holy goals and in retreat from God?

I say unto you, I say unto you verily: you must search your heart with detachment and willpower, with truth and honesty, and, above all, with patience and attention to detail. For every thought, every emotion, every action in your life will be the subject of a complete review at the time of the judgment of God after the passage that is death.

Are you in a state of holiness with regard to every thought, every emotion, every action of your life? No? Then you must submit everything—absolutely everything—that is not holy before God the Father Almighty. Is this duty too large? Too complex? Yes, surely. That is why I hasten to your aid! The powers of redemption contained within my stigmata, by virtue of the Sacrament of confession, will perform miracles of absolution for you.

Alleluia! Alleluia! Alleluia! Blessed are those who are invited to the blessing of the Sacrament of confession, testimony of the infinite love and infinite mercy of God the Father, the Creator of us all. Amen. Alleluia!

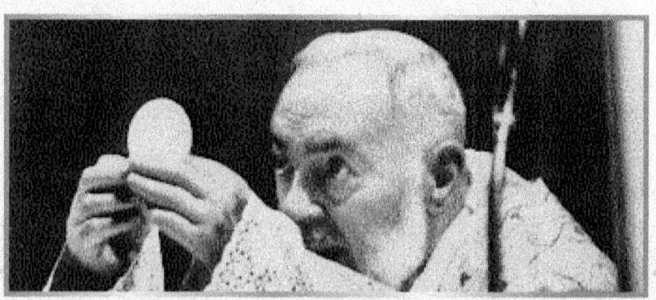

SAINT PADRE PIO

Speaks

SAINT PADRE PIO

Speaks

Chapter 10

My children of the promised earth, I bless you, in the Name of the Father, and of the Son, and of the Holy Spirit. The confession that you will soon receive is part of your redemption. However, your redemption consists of many aspects of a new heart: conversion to Christ Jesus, the will to transform your own heart, regularly repeated confession, actual practice of the teachings of Christ in your life, and, above all, diffusion of the Word of God around you.

It is critical at this point in the course of humanity to take an active and engaged position so that the mercy being granted to you multiplies and leads to the conversion of many souls around you. This miraculous book has reached you today to aid you in proceeding with the complete and glorious salvation of your soul. It has also reached you because your redemption will in turn allow the redemption of countless souls.

Indeed, it has been determined that you belong to a key junction of a human network to which it pleases God to offer His infinite mercy. Your soul is like a cosmic pivot that will sway the justice of God towards humanity— at least in part, and perhaps even in its entirety! Do not underestimate the value of the redemption of your single soul. In the Eyes of God the Father, a soul as white as snow can cleanse the debts of all humanity... if it so pleases the Father.

Alleluia! Alleluia! Alleluia! Blessed are the Apostles of the Good News of God the Father, for God the Father reserves His Kingdom for those who proclaim and honor His Holy and Glorious Name across the entire earth. Amen. Alleluia!

SAINT PADRE PIO

Speaks

SAINT PADRE PIO

Speaks

Chapter 11

My little children, come into my arms! Nothing on earth can truly console you. Nothing among men can be offered to you that will give you peace. True peace, lasting and profound, exists only in Christ Jesus, our Savior and our God.

The stigmata that I still bear are the emblem of my cosmic fusion with Christ Jesus in all His energetic aspects. My stigmata reflect my Christification, that is to say, my total transformation in Christic energy. Christ Jesus is the Christ Master of all the souls who have become christified: for Him, by Him, through Him, in virtue of Him, and in His Holy and Great Name.

Come into my arms, therefore, and find the peace of Christ! I bless you in the Name of the Father, and of the Son, and of Holy Spirit. Amen. Alleluia!

SAINT PADRE PIO

Speaks

Chapter 12

My children, listen to me well. Confession is a Holy Sacrament introduced among men by our Lord Jesus. When He taught the Apostles about the matters of repentance, He introduced the elements of confession, that is to say, sincere contrition of the sinful heart, admission of sins before God the Father, and willingness to transform one's human heart into a Divine heart.

That is the profound value of confession: the willingness to be transformed, a fundamental principle that emerges only if the soul truly recognizes its sins and repents proportionately. Repentance without willingness to be transformed is vain and useless. Would it please God our Father to observe His child repeat the same mistakes and offenses endlessly and without growth of the spirit? Of course not! It is necessary that the heart be transformed by chasing away the darkness within it in order to accept the Light of Christ.

Alleluia! Alleluia! Alleluia! Blessed is he who understands the foundation of the holy confession accomplished before God the Father, who knows everything. Amen. Alleluia!

SAINT PADRE PIO

Speaks

Chapter 13

My dear children, be firm in your faith, always, and be firm in your belief in the life in the Kingdom of God awaiting you. Turn away from teachings that talk about latent transitional states in the ethereal dimensions of the universe after the passage that is death.

I say unto you, I say unto you verily, the Kingdom of Heaven is real and marvelous, and I want to come to greet you, to welcome you and hold you in my arms at the time of your royal entrance among us after the passage that is death. What rejoicing there is here in Paradise when a beautiful soul finally joins us!

I pray with all my heart for the salvation of your soul, so that you are not forced to be exiled in purgatory. The Legion of Saint Paul—to which all of us here belong—will continue to guide you and protect you.

I love you so much. I am Saint Padre Pio and I love you so much!

Alleluia! Alleluia! Alleluia! Blessed is he who prepares for his death during every moment of his life. Amen. Alleluia!

SAINT PADRE PIO

Speaks

SAINT PADRE PIO

Speaks

Chapter 14

My children, be patient in your approach to God. Whatever elements arise in your life remain in a state of gratitude toward God. Through everything and at all times, each circumstance, each individual, and each problem has been wisely and lovingly chosen for the sake of your spiritual advancement and your return to the peace of God. Why be anxious? Why be angry? Why be unhappy?

I say unto you, I say unto you verily: God the Father makes all decisions about whatever concerns the tiniest details of your life, the life of each and every one of you, and He never leaves anything to chance. Be reassured, therefore, that the road you walk at this time of your life is well-known—not only to God the Father, but also to all of us in Heaven, including Christ Jesus our Lord and our God, the Holy Spirit, your Guardian Angel, all the Saints of Paradise, and all the Angels of God.

For your life is precious in the Eyes of God, who sees everything, who hears everything, who knows everything, and who, above all, creates everything at every moment and in every place, in all the dimensions of the visible and invisible universe.

Alleluia! Alleluia! Alleluia! Blessed is he who gives himself with joy and gratitude to the supreme Will of God the Father, Creator of everything. Amen. Alleluia!

SAINT PADRE PIO

Speaks

SAINT PADRE PIO
Speaks

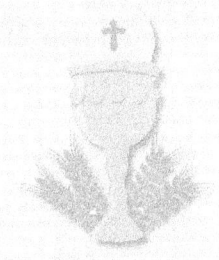

Chapter 15

My children, my children, be happy, for I have entered your life. I, Saint Padre Pio, the man purified by the grace of God the Father, the man sacrificed by the love of Christ, the man who became Saint by Divine Mercy, am now at your side forever, world without end.

Call unto me, invoke me, ask for my intercession in your requests and petitions before God the Father Most High, and I will be elated and eager to work very hard for you. For the salvation of your soul is all that matters to me, now that your life has been assigned to me by the blessed Providence.

I am there, I will always be there, and I love you so much. I am Saint Padre Pio and I love you!

Alleluia! Alleluia! Alleluia! Blessed is he who hears my words of love and throws himself into my arms, for my devotion to him will be eternal. Amen. Alleluia!

Chapter 16

My children, I am pleased to speak to you today, for God the Father has given me His agreement so that I may prepare your soul for a beautiful confession, complete and genuine.

You see, the Holy Sacrament of confession is critical and necessary for the cosmic redemption of your soul. The confession is much more than a session for enumerating sins and regrettable actions. Of course not! Holy Confession, which is pleasing to God the Father Creator, includes a firm and sincere willingness to transform oneself completely, to change one's human heart into a Divine heart by achieving an inner discipline and the resulting novel behavior.

God expects spiritual progress and a contrite heart, so that you may attain purification of the soul, elimination of the ego, and perfection in the way of living created by Him with love.

Let us give glory to God the Father through our deep and true consent to submit to a confession before Him, a confession that is salutary for the soul and redeeming through the sacred Blood of the Lamb of God, the Savior of us all, our Lord Jesus Christ, the unique source of Peace.

Alleluia! Alleluia! Alleluia! Blessed is the one who prepares for a true and genuine confession before God the Father Almighty, for I, Saint Padre Pio of Pietrelcina, will be there and will assist Him. Amen. Alleluia!

SAINT PADRE PIO

Speaks

Chapter 17

My children, I say unto you, I say unto you verily: the situation is serious. It is impossible to adequately describe the events that are fast approaching. Remain on constant alert! Days and nights are already being counted that will bring us to the Great Cosmic Day inaugurating the extraordinarily difficult but necessary transition.

Get ready today. I urge you to begin your personal and spiritual process of redemption before God the Eternal Father. For this intimate and painful examination of mistakes and offenses cannot be postponed until tomorrow.

A detailed and genuine exploration of all aspects of the past, including every thought, every emotion, every action that you have experienced and that is recorded in the archives of your life, cannot be accomplished without our divine help. The work involved is too heavy and complicated, the

possibility of denial too paralyzing, the justification too easy, and the inner and outer obstacles too numerous for a single human soul to cope with. Therefore, I offer my services as divine confessor appointed to the salvation of your soul, and I shall make your soul as beautiful and as white as snow before God the Father Almighty after the passage that is death.

I do not know the date and time of your death. But I do know that time passes quickly on earth. And I know that the difficult events that are approaching will not allow the survival of all humans currently living. I shall stop here. . . .

Suffice it to say that the Eternal Father loves you and has lifted His merciful Eyes unto you. The proof is within this miraculous book in your hands. For as of this very day and for the rest of your life, and forever, world without end, I shall be there with you. I shall attend to your inner work of complete and genuine redemption, and we will celebrate with joyfulness your royal entrance in the Kingdom of Heaven that is awaiting you. I love you so much.

Alleluia! Alleluia! Alleluia! Blessed is he who reads this miraculous book blessed by God, for Saint Padre Pio enters your life, today, for the salvation of your beloved soul. Amen. Alleluia!

SAINT PADRE PIO

Speaks

SAINT PADRE PIO

Speaks

Chapter 18

My children, I am here in Heaven, and I am there in your heart, no matter where you are and what you are doing. I am always there with you, day and night. I assist you, I encourage you, and I guide you at all times, regardless of whether I am in your mind or not. My presence in your heart is eternal, ineffable, and intimate, as real as if you and I were joined at the hip.

My presence in your life will be increasingly felt throughout your awakening of consciousness, which is heightening day by day. Soon you will be able to retain my image and my unique influence in your heart, allowing you to accelerate your spiritual progress.

I have been called to energetically join myself to you by virtue of the infinite mercy of God the Father toward your soul. Honor and praise to God the Father for so much love poured into your life right now!

Verily, verily, I say unto you, I am there in your heart in a more powerful way than you can imagine, and your gratitude before God the Father Creator will be boundless and will only deepen.

Alleluia! Alleluia! Alleluia! Blessed are the souls chosen by God Himself, called to read this miraculous book and to live in the divine and providential company of the Saints in Paradise. Amen. Alleluia!

SAINT PADRE PIO

Speaks

Chapter 19

My children, always remain in the Light of Christ! Christ Jesus, my Savior and my God, is the Light of the world! He is the Light of all the worlds known and unknown to men! Here in Paradise, Christ Jesus is King with His Father and the Holy Spirit. The Christic light is dazzling with beauty, power, and love, beyond any possible illustration using the words of the intellect.

Alleluia! Alleluia! Alleluia! Blessed is he who comes in the name of the Lord, for the Light of Christ is in him! Amen. Alleluia!

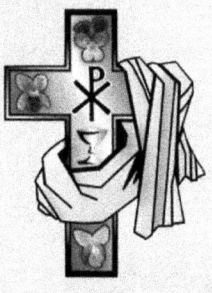

SAINT PADRE PIO

Speaks

Chapter 20

My dear children, I am there in your heart and I experience the joys and sorrows of your life, the dramas of your daily existence, your disappointments and your hopes. Your life is perfectly and totally visible to us, the inhabitants of Paradise, even if this seems difficult for you to imagine.

Your physical and temporal dimension is fluid, and it is permeable to our entering and leaving as we please; this is why we can visit you, observe you, circulate with you here and there (whether you are on foot or traveling by car, plane, or boat). Above all, we can guide you, inspire you, and comfort you, for we are divine benefactors and will never abandon you.

Alleluia! Alleluia! Alleluia! Blessed is he who receives the visitations of the Saints of Paradise and the Angels of God, for graces, miracles, and abundance will be brought to him. Amen. Alleluia!

SAINT PADRE PIO

Speaks

Chapter 21

My children, be reassured in knowing that your soul is well-nestled in my hands. I will never abandon you, I will always comfort you, I will guide you every step of your life, and I will bring you to confession regularly—sometimes with the help of a human priest.

Your contrition before God, made in the intimacy of your heart and with my assistance, pleases God. This unique grace of confession, which was given to me (and for which I am immensely thankful to the Almighty), is now given to you so that you may proceed to the salvation of your soul.

A confession on your part made in the intimacy of your heart, wherever you are and assisted by my divine intercession, moves you gradually toward the Kingdom of God. Do not neglect to visit your parish priest, however, in order to comply with the rituals of the Church.

Make me your spiritual and personal confessor before God, in the secret of your heart! Be at peace, knowing that Saint Padre Pio of Pietrelcina is your confessor, appointed by God Himself—for God Himself is the One who led you to read this book blessed by Him.

Verily, verily, I say unto you, your confession, made now before God and with my intercession, means infinite mercy before God, as truly and tangibly as if we were together in my confessional in San Giovanni Rotondo.

God does not get old, God does not change, God hears my prayers and your confession in the same way that He heard them when I was a Capuchin Father living on earth. But the power of my stigmata was amplified when I entered Paradise.

Verily, verily I say unto you, make an intimate confession often before God the Father with my divine intercession; make a formal confession often with a priest on earth . . . and with all that, God the Father will be pleased. Amen. Alleluia!

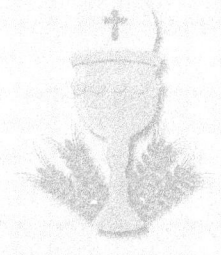

Chapter 22

My beloved children, I am bringing you today to confession. Your soul is in my hands, now and forever, world without end. Today is a crucial and blissful moment in the history of your soul. The Holy Sacrament of Confession is a majestic gift, cosmic and marvelous, offered by God the Father Almighty in order to give your soul an opportunity to atone for your sins before Him.

All that you need is your awareness of yourself. Drop all of your earthly concerns. Remember that, in truth, God is preoccupied only with your soul. Now, take a look back and gather in your heart all of your mistakes and offenses committed against God and your fellow men during the course of your life. Bow down before God the Father Almighty, stripped from any corporal envelope and stripped of any physical resistance, with your heart repentant and contrite for so many injustices done against the Holy Trinity and men.

With the simple and humble spirit of a little child who can do nothing without his parents, the mind clear and in recollection pacifying itself in the very Source of Peace, simply say: "God, my Eternal Father, I committed the following sins [list here your deepest secrets], and I promise you from the bottom of my heart not to offend you further in any way whatever. If I fall again, I promise to be back here before You, twice as humble and contrite, and I will renew my promise with even more faith and determination. My Father, my God, my Creator, forgive me my sins, through the bleeding and triumphant wounds of our Lord Jesus Christ and the Immaculate Heart of Mary. Saint Padre Pio, pray for me. Amen."

Alleluia! Alleluia! Alleluia! Blessed is the soul who confesses today, for today God the Father Almighty opens His Arms wide to your repentant soul and engraves infinite mercy for the salvation of your soul in His Great Plan of Salvation for humanity. Amen. Alleluia!

SAINT PADRE PIO

Speaks

Chapter 23

My children, I carry you in my heart for the rest of your life—and beyond. When I lived in San Giovanni Rotondo, assisting the souls that the Heavenly Father sent me every day for their redemption, I never expected that my mission would continue after my death. In fact, my mission has not only been extended, it has been intensified, and it is blessed with a formidable and cosmic power.

For I have become a Christ, like all the other Saints of Paradise, through the imitation of Christ, which I experienced at all levels during my journey on earth.

I am in a state of immense reverence and elation because I am living here in Paradise with Christ Jesus, my King and my God, the Blessed Virgin Mary, the Holy Spirit, the Father Creator Almighty, and among the Celestial Court, rejoicing in an ineffable and incomparable beatitude at all times.

I am also thankful to all the souls who visited me during my journey on earth. When making the effort to travel to and meet me in San Giovanni Rotondo, these souls obeyed the inspiration of the Holy Spirit, who operates according to God's Plan of Salvation. These souls contributed to the salvation of my own soul by giving me the opportunity to put into action the graces of cosmic redemption and divine confession that had been given to me by God the Father Himself!

I also wish to testify that I hear and listen with compassion to all the prayers and petitions made through my intercession, and I carry them assiduously and with joy and exaltation to God the Father. For my current power here above is greater than it was in the past down below, and innumerable miracles and blessings await you when you ask for my intercession before God the Father for anything you may need.

Alleluia! Alleluia! Alleluia! Blessed is he who prays to God through my intercession, for the treasures of Paradise are theirs! Amen. Alleluia!

Chapter 24

My children, the persecution that I suffered from my superiors for many years was, in fact, very beneficial for the elevation of my soul toward God.

These trials and tribulations, these restrictions in relation to my duties as a priest, were allowed by God the Loving Father in order to purify my soul and to increase my faith in Him and intensify the fervor of my prayers to Him, through Christ Jesus, my Lord, and the Immaculate Heart of Mary, my Mother.

The human souls who participated in the evil plots against me had been victims of manipulation by the devil; they had been used without their knowledge. The human ego— the collection of errors and negativity that invade human thoughts and emotions—is directly connected to the demon who wishes the fall of Christ and the domination of darkness upon the earth.

Do not be seduced by the forces of the demon when negative suggestions invade you. Pray instead! If you are persecuted, pray even harder, asking God for strength and courage to win this internal struggle and to quickly arrive on the other side of this phase of difficult teaching permitted by God Himself. God the Father wishes to see your soul as pure and white as snow, fortified by a strong and solid faith anchored only in Him!

SAINT PADRE PIO

Speaks

SAINT PADRE PIO

Speaks

Chapter 25

My beloved children, I am pleased to tell you about my childhood. When my father moved to the United States of America to work, my mother and I spent a lot of time talking, bonding, and healing the loneliness caused by his absence.

But my mother revealed herself to be a soul much more spiritually advanced than my little child's eyes could have suspected. In truth, the Blessed Virgin Mary, in all Her benevolence towards me, proved Herself to me in the beginning through the tenderness and the maternal love of my mother.

My intimacy with my mother grew because of my intimacy with the Most Blessed Virgin Mary; and, proportionately, my intimacy with the Most Blessed Virgin Mary was deepened by the love of my own mother. Do you see?

The union of the child and his mother is critical to the spiritual development of the soul that journeys towards God. The Tenderness of Mary, the Love of Mary, the Immaculate Heart of Mary, my Queen, allowed me to get here, to the Kingdom of Heaven where I live and from where I am writing to you today.

Pray my children, pray to the Very Good and Salutary Virgin Mary, and she will perform miracles in your life! Amen. Alleluia!

SAINT PADRE PIO

Speaks

SAINT PADRE PIO

Speaks

Chapter 26

My children, I want to talk to you about your Guardian Angel. Your Guardian Angel is always with you, loves you and protects you, and leads you gently toward God the Father in his capacity as an Angel.

An Angel is a messenger of God. This Angel always communicates with God on your behalf. He receives instructions from God the Father for your benefit, and He performs His duties with precision and perfection, for He is the pure Light of God.

The Angel also prays on your behalf in order to speed your return to God the Father. He rejoices in your progress, He is saddened by your mistakes and sins—but He does not judge you. The Angel has no ego, no darkness. He is Love of God, Light of God, Life of God, and His intentions toward you are entirely divine.

Pray often to your Guardian Angel. Tell him: "My good Angel, I love you; keep me very close to you, and lead me quickly into the loving Arms of God the Father without offending Him and without offending my fellow men. Amen." Alleluia!

During my life on earth, I developed a very intimate relationship with my Angel. He performed many services for me, and He has contributed to the salvation of my soul. I pray that you awaken yourself today to the love and divine powers of your Guardian Angel. Amen. Alleluia!

SAINT PADRE PIO

Speaks

SAINT PADRE PIO

Speaks

Chapter 27

My children, my children, listen to me well. It is said that a fragrance of violet is associated with my presence when I am near you. I wish to confirm this phenomenon of the Holy Spirit. Indeed, this fragrance is associated with the exquisite emanations from the Blood and Wounds of Christ, my Savior and my God. My blood has joined with His Blood in the superior dimensions of the cosmos.

However, I would also like to make clear that my being near you is not always associated with a scent; so do not doubt my presence when there is no fragrance or other signs of it. Be assured that I am with you, always and everywhere, and that I am with you for the rest of your life—and beyond.

I love you. . . . I am Saint Padre Pio of Pietrelcina and I love you! Amen!

Chapter 28

My beloved children, the House for the Relief of the Suffering has been the most precious project of my life. What triumph in adversity! What tangible evidence of the power of faith, work, perseverance, and prayer carried out in pursuit of a purposeful and edifying goal!

I visit this hospital every day because of the countless prayers that are presented to me from inside the walls of this beloved institution. I hasten and am delighted to help all those who ask for my help and intercession and who are at the House for the Relief of the Suffering—and everywhere else. The tears, the suffering, and the despair of the souls who seek me touch me deeply and equally, regardless of their location and the spiritual state of their souls.

The stigmata I bear allow the complete redemption of all souls seeking the infinite mercy found therein, the ineffable grace of the Loving and Almighty God.

Thanks be to God for the miracle that is the House for the Relief of the Suffering and for the infinite mercy that is hiding within the stigmata, available to all who are seeking it. Amen. Alleluia!

SAINT PADRE PIO

Speaks

Chapter 29

My children, I bless you in the Name of the Father, and of the Son, and of the Holy Spirit. Few things in your life have value in the Eyes of God, the Father of us all. Your soul, stripped of the corporeal envelope, detached from any social attribute, your soul considered in isolation is the only part of you in which the Father is interested. For your soul is your truth, made in the image and likeness of God.

Take care of your soul. Do not damage it by harmful and addictive activities that invite the ego to submerge you in darkness; do not ignore it by worrying too much about your body image; do not invest any emotion in money or in social status, for God takes no interest in these.

And above all, submit your soul to the scalpel of confession in order to extract thereby the residue of offenses and

mistakes made against God and men. For God wishes to see in you a soul as white as snow, cleansed and purified of all thoughts, emotions, and actions that have been imperfect and unholy in His Eyes.

I am there with you, and I will help you prepare your soul to meet God. Amen.

SAINT PADRE PIO

Speaks

Chapter 30

My children, I am pleased to speak to you today about childhood. Few children in the world today are interested in Christ Jesus or in turning toward God.

Unfortunately, life on earth is centered on the acquisition of goods, entertainment of body and spirit, idleness, and ease. So many errors are written into the lives of our young people! Intellectual laziness, dangerous adventures, and fluctuating emotions create a psychological context very destructive to the spiritual growth of our children.

I recommend that parents bring their small children to Church from an early age, despite their lack of discipline during mass, and expose them as early and as quickly as possible to the teachings of Christ and to religious rituals.

Christ Jesus Himself will come into their hearts and guide them the rest of the way. But we must first introduce them to Christ in order to allow the rapid spiritual opening performed by Jesus, who so much loves youth, full of promise and hope.

Dear parents, pursue the work of spiritualizing your child with hope and persistence, and Jesus Himself will do the rest. For today's child will be the child of a New Sun very shortly, a child of Christ. Amen. Alleluia!

SAINT PADRE PIO

Speaks

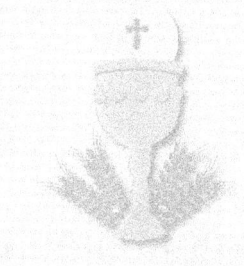

Chapter 31

My children, I am able to perform miracles for you at all levels in order to accomplish anything whatsoever, and no problem is too difficult for me to overcome. The miracles obtained through the intercession of the Saints in Paradise reach earth to produce practical and tangible benefits: the healing of the sick, the return of a lost child, the relief of financial difficulties, and so on.

From the perspective of Heaven, these favors and benevolent graces are not at all complex or grandiose in their execution. Here in Paradise, the desire of God the Father is fulfilled instantly, and what pleases Him simply is.

No time need elapse and no elaborate discussions need take place before a prayer is granted. In His ineffable Wisdom

and in His Power incomprehensible to humans, God the Father sees everything, hears everything, knows everything, and decides everything, at all times, with regard to all His creatures on earth.

What pleases God the Father is done without employing the means of time and space; His Will is Reality, His Will is Truth, His Will is.

Glory be to God in the Highest Heaven, and peace on earth to men of good will! Amen. Alleluia!

SAINT PADRE PIO

Speaks

SAINT PADRE PIO
Speaks

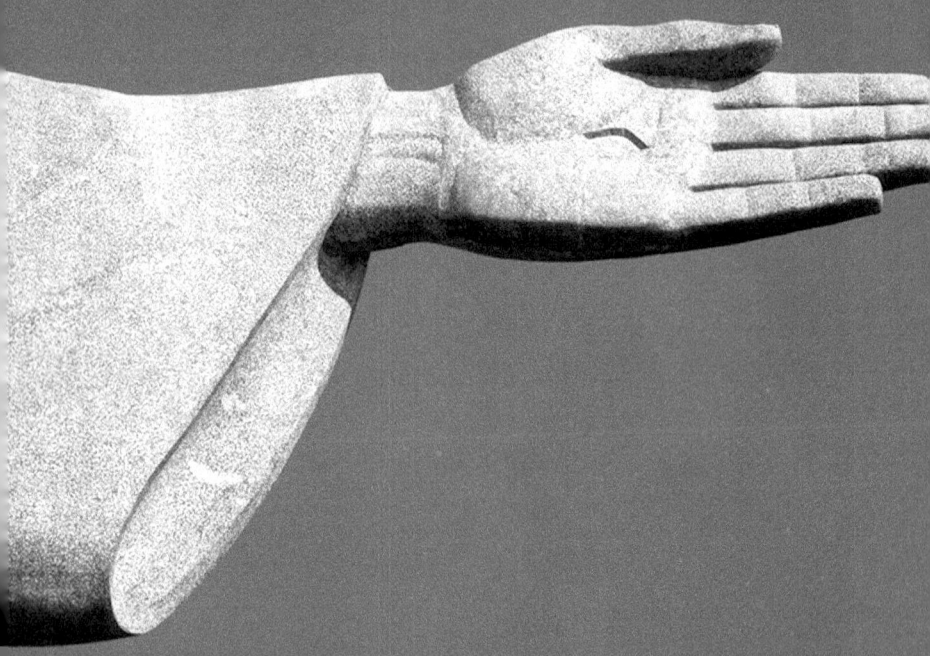

Chapter 32

My children, my beloved children of the earth, I embrace you very affectionately. I shall hold you in my arms and in my heart forever. Make a path of redemption to God the Father Almighty and request the Divine and Infinite Mercy of God for your soul, the soul of a sinner. I will assist you always, whether you call me or not. I will always be there in virtue of the magnetic bond that unites us now. This bond has been established, consolidated, and sealed for Eternity, through this book blessed by God that you have in your hands.

For this book, miraculous of divine grace, has been authorized and conceived by God the Father Almighty Himself. I have endless gratitude to the Father, our Creator, and to His Son, our Savior.

Alleluia! Alleluia! Alleluia! Blessed, blessed by God, is he who reads this book and who applies the divine instruction given herein, for redemption of the soul is initiated and accelerated by Saint Padre Pio of Pietrelcina. Amen. Alleluia!

I love you so much. I will speak to you again soon.

I bless you in the Name of the Father, and of the Son, and of the Holy Spirit. Amen.

Saint Padre Pio of Pietrelcina

SAINT PADRE PIO

Speaks

Afterword

Pio visits me every Friday morning. Every Friday is the day of the Passion of our Lord and Savior. He is the living room when I wake up. He greets me after I am dressed properly, watches me get my coffee and have breakfast, we chit chat and discuss internal news and global affairs, then we pray together. Always too prematurely, he hugs me one last time and he disappears. Among all the Saints who visit me, Pio gives the best bear hugs!

May Pio visit you as often as he visits me.

Pio, I love you!

In Jesus and Mary, Marie-Josée

About The Author

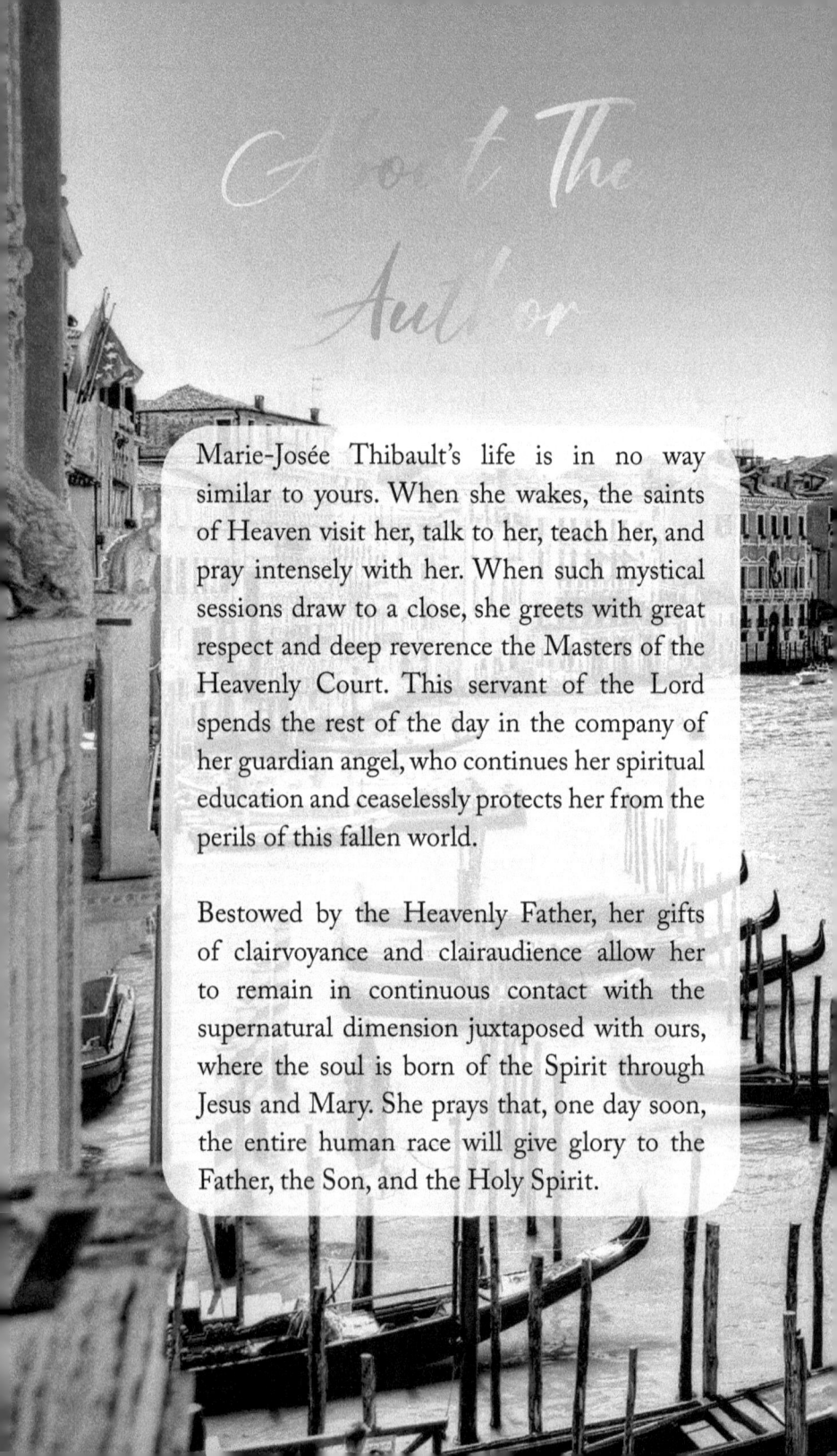

Marie-Josée Thibault's life is in no way similar to yours. When she wakes, the saints of Heaven visit her, talk to her, teach her, and pray intensely with her. When such mystical sessions draw to a close, she greets with great respect and deep reverence the Masters of the Heavenly Court. This servant of the Lord spends the rest of the day in the company of her guardian angel, who continues her spiritual education and ceaselessly protects her from the perils of this fallen world.

Bestowed by the Heavenly Father, her gifts of clairvoyance and clairaudience allow her to remain in continuous contact with the supernatural dimension juxtaposed with ours, where the soul is born of the Spirit through Jesus and Mary. She prays that, one day soon, the entire human race will give glory to the Father, the Son, and the Holy Spirit.

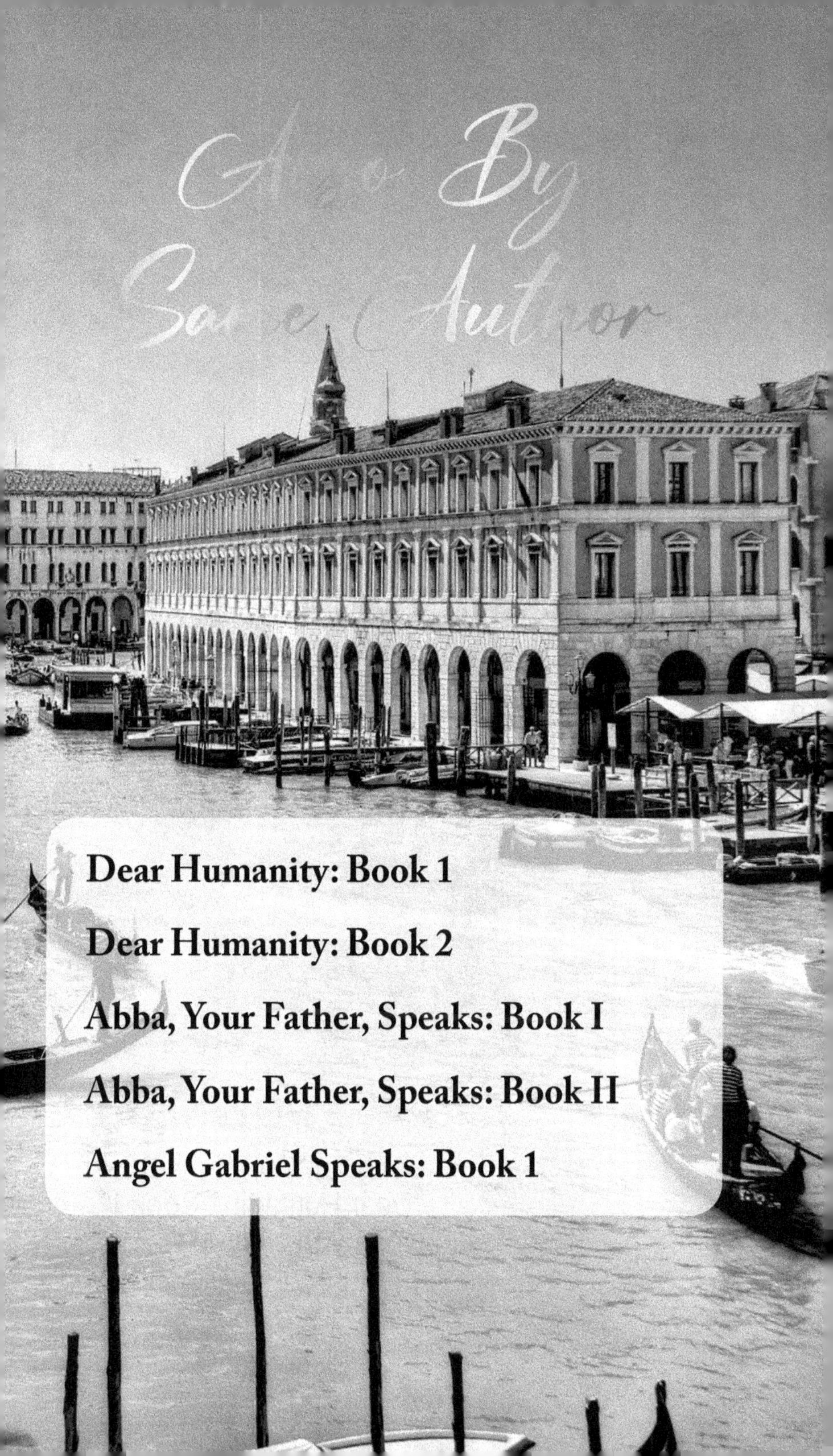

Also By Same Author

Dear Humanity: Book 1

Dear Humanity: Book 2

Abba, Your Father, Speaks: Book I

Abba, Your Father, Speaks: Book II

Angel Gabriel Speaks: Book 1

FREE DOWNLOAD

Get your free copy of :
"Dear Humanity: Book 1"
when you sign up to the
author's VIP mailing list!
Get started here:

www.abbamyfatheriloveyou.com

www.ingramcontent.com/pod-product-compliance
Lightning Source LLC
Chambersburg PA
CBHW070504100426
42743CB00010B/1758